D1398954

Little Bible Heroes™
Miriam

Written by Victoria Kovacs
Illustrated by Mike Krome

B&H KIDS
NASHVILLE, TENNESSEE

GOLDQUILL
WWW.GOLDQUILL.CO.UK

Published by B&H Publishing Group 2015. Text and illustrations copyright © 2014, GoldQuill, United Kingdom.
All rights reserved. Scripture quotations are taken from the Holman Christian Standard Bible ® Copyright © 1999, 2000, 2002, 2003,
2009 by Holman Bible Publishers. Used by permission. Printed in Heshan, Guangdong, China, June 2017
ISBN: 978-1-4336-8717-4   Dewey Decimal Classification: CE
Subject Heading: MIRIAM \ DANIEL \ BIBLE STORIES
4 5 6 7 8 9 • 21 20 19 18 17

The ruler of Egypt is an
evil pharaoh who orders
all the Hebrew baby boys
to be killed. One mother
has a plan to protect her
baby boy. She makes a
papyrus basket, coats it
with clay and tar to make
it float, and places the
baby inside.

The mother and her daughter, Miriam, put the basket in the reeds along the riverbank. They pray for God to take care of their baby.

Miriam is a very brave big sister.
She hides and watches over her
brother's floating basket.

Pharaoh's daughter comes to the river to take a bath. She sees the basket and looks inside.

Miriam is worried. What will the princess do to her little brother?

The princess picks up the basket and says, "I will take care of this baby as my own."

Miriam runs to the princess and asks bravely, "Would you like me to find a nurse for the baby?"

"Yes," answers the princess.

Miriam is happy. Now her brother is safe! She takes him home so their mother can be his nurse. The baby stays with his real family a little while longer.

When Miriam's brother is older, their mother brings him to the princess. The princess names him Moses. Moses grows up to become a great leader of his people.

Read:

When the child grew older, she brought him to Pharaoh's daughter, and he became her son. She named him Moses, "Because," she said, "I drew him out of the water."—Exodus 2:10

Think:

1. Has God ever protected you from trouble?
2. How was Miriam brave? When have you been brave?

Remember:

I will both lie down and sleep in peace, for You alone, LORD, make me live in safety.
—Psalm 4:8

Read:

Then the king promoted Daniel and gave him many generous gifts. He made him ruler over the entire province of Babylon and chief governor over all the wise men of Babylon.—Daniel 2:48

Think:

1. Is it hard to obey God when others tell you not to?
2. Daniel prayed to God for help. When has God answered your prayers and helped you?

Remember:

The LORD is far from the wicked, but He hears the prayer of the righteous.—Proverbs 15:29

Years later, wicked men throw Daniel into a den of lions because he prayed to God instead of to the new king. God sends an angel to shut the lions' mouths. Daniel is saved!

The king now knows that Daniel's God is the one true God. To show his thanks, the king gives Daniel gifts and makes him a ruler over the country.

Daniel quickly goes to
the king and explains
what God had told him.
The king is very happy
to know what his dreams
mean.

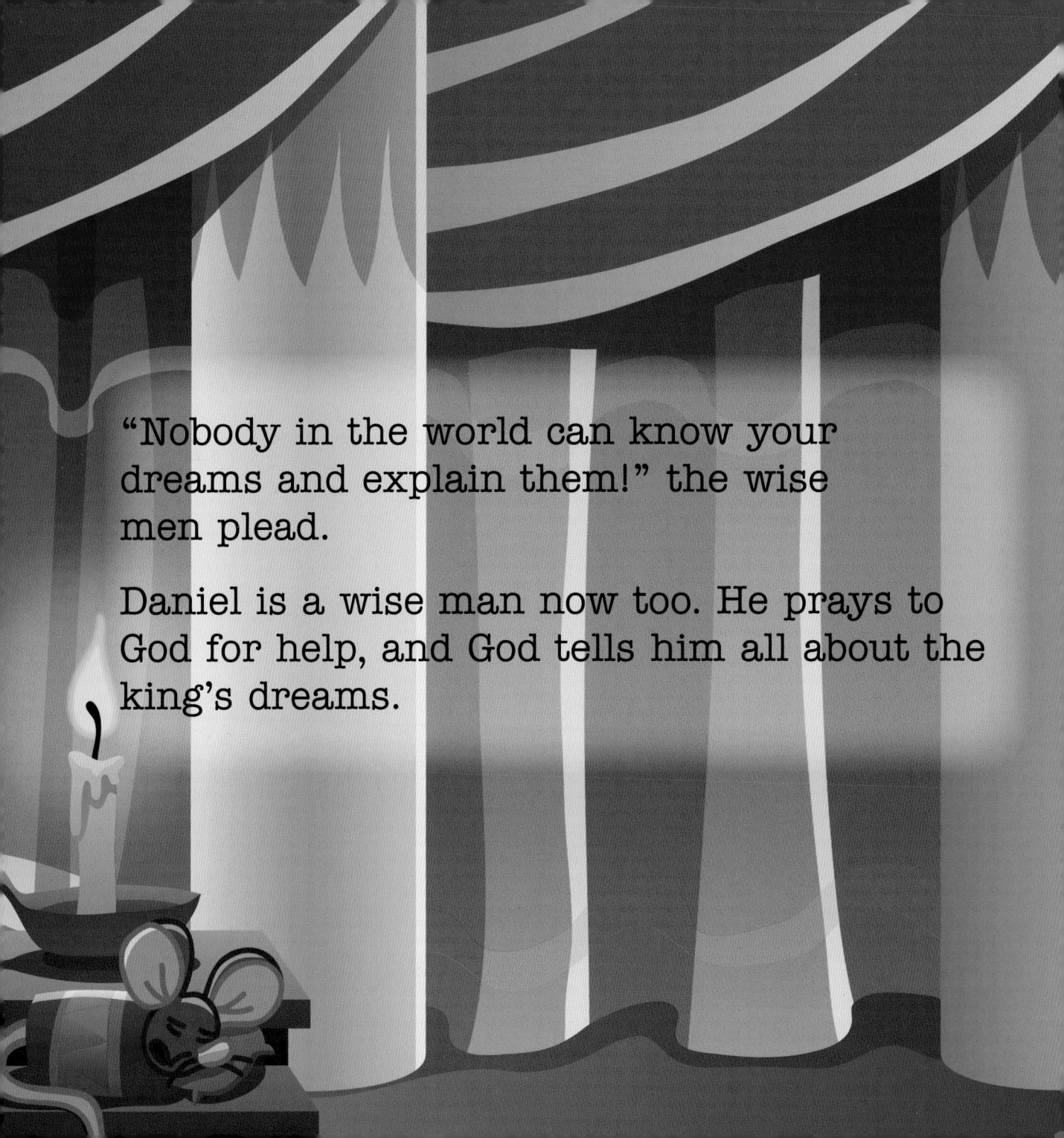

"Nobody in the world can know your dreams and explain them!" the wise men plead.

Daniel is a wise man now too. He prays to God for help, and God tells him all about the king's dreams.

Later, the king has terrible dreams. He orders all the wise men put to death because they can't tell him what he dreamed and what the dreams mean.

They are given unhealthy food and wine, but Daniel and his friends keep God's laws and choose vegetables and water instead. After ten days, they look healthier than the others and are allowed to keep obeying God's laws.

Daniel is a young man in Israel.
When the king of Babylon conquers
the city of Jerusalem, he takes
Daniel and his friends to his palace
to work as his servants.

Little Bible Heroes™
Daniel

Written by Victoria Kovacs
Illustrated by David Ryley

**BH
KIDS**

NASHVILLE, TENNESSEE

GOLDQUILL
WWW.GOLDQUILL.CO.UK

Published by B&H Publishing Group 2015. Text and illustrations copyright © 2014, GoldQuill, United Kingdom.
All rights reserved. Scripture quotations are taken from the Holman Christian Standard Bible ® Copyright © 1999, 2000, 2002, 2003, 2009 by Holman Bible Publishers. Used by permission. Printed in Heshan, Guangdong, China, June 2017
ISBN: 978-1-4336-8717-4   Dewey Decimal Classification: CE
Subject Heading: MIRIAM \ DANIEL \ BIBLE STORIES
4 5 6 7 8 9 • 21 20 19 18 17